Usborne Early Years Wipe-clean
Numbers
1 to 10

Add 10 dots to my sail.

Illustrated by
Damien and Lisa Barlow

7

8

9

10

Written by
Jessica
Greenwell

Designed by
Stephanie
Jeffries and
Claire Ever

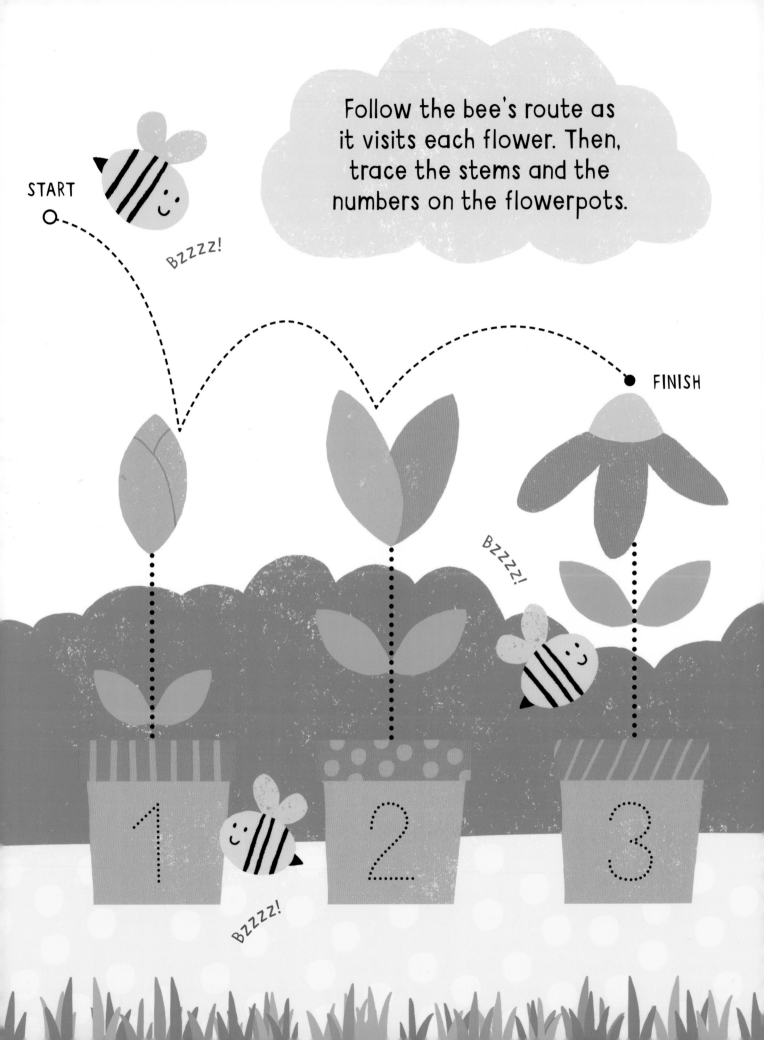

START

Bzzzz!

Follow the bee's route as it visits each flower. Then, trace the stems and the numbers on the flowerpots.

FINISH

Bzzzz!

Bzzzz!

1

2

3

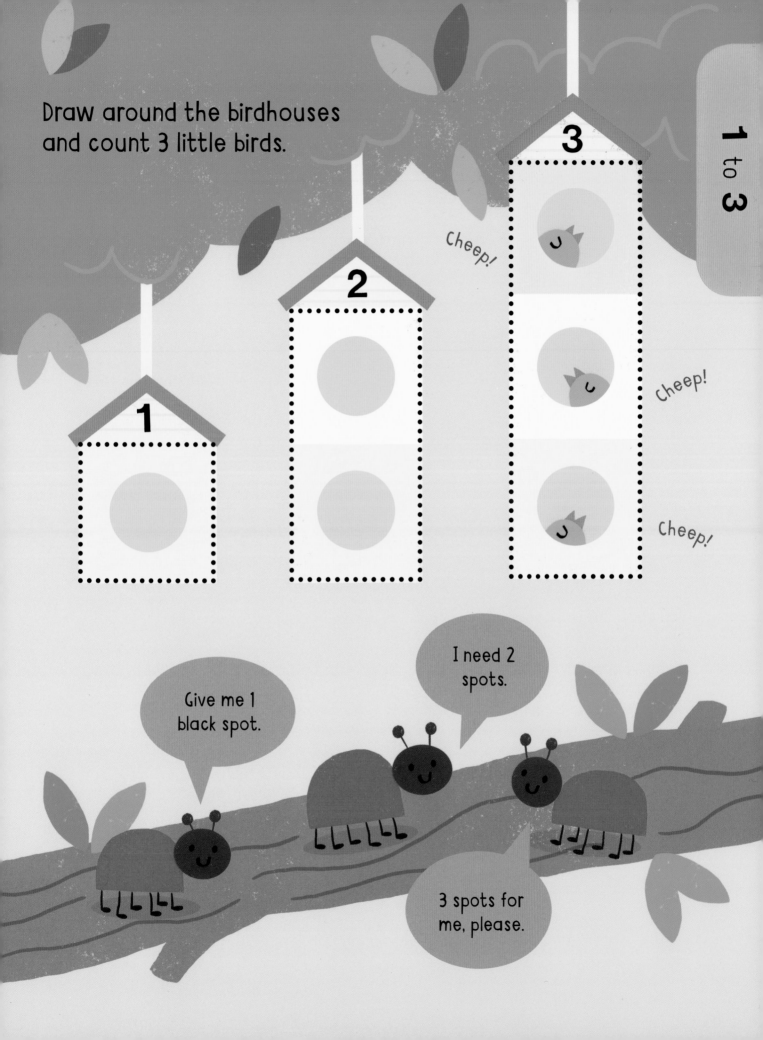

Trace the trail the snail has left through the garden.

1 Pumpkin

START

3 Carrots

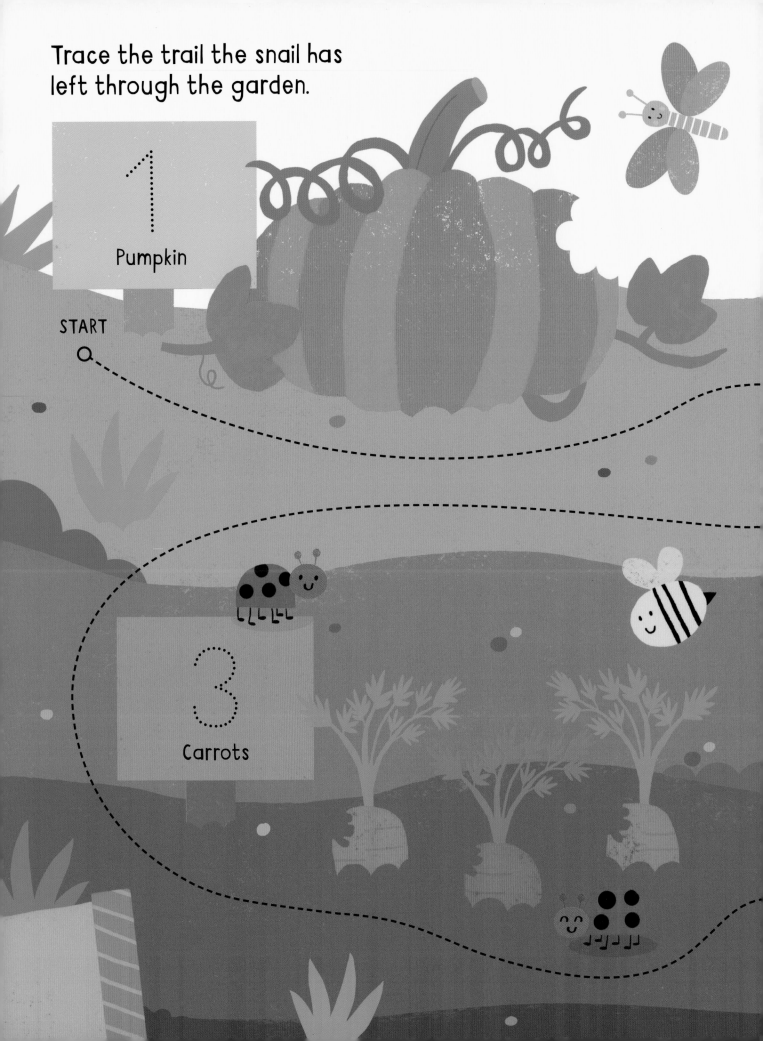

Count the boats below and trace the numbers, starting at number 1.

Help Cat deliver the letters. Trace the numbers on the envelopes then draw lines to match them to the correct doors, starting with number 1.

Count the number of things in each shop window.

Find and circle 6 birds.

TOYS

FRUIT & VEGETABLES

Books

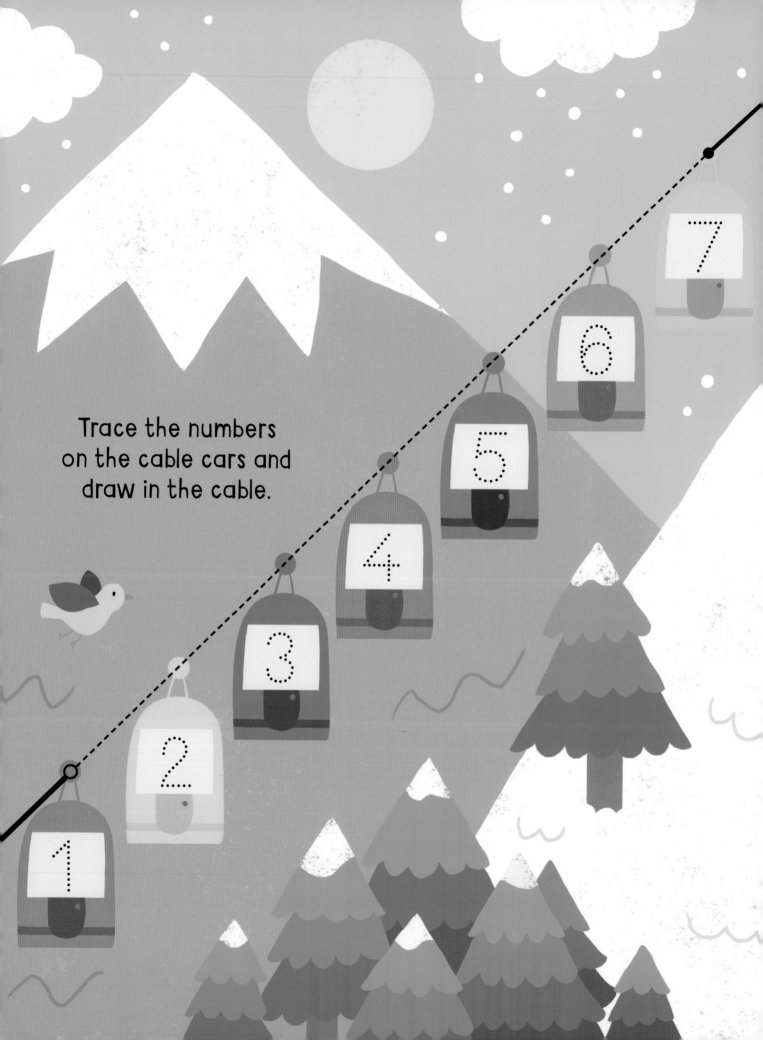

Trace the numbers on the cable cars and draw in the cable.

Trace the numbers on the 8 balloons.

Show the animals how to cross
the river by tracing the route
across the stepping stones.

Can you spot and circle 8 dragonflies?

5

6

7

8

6 7 8 9

Can you find and circle 9 birds?

...and trace around each one.

5 6 7 8 9

Draw the route of the ball around this mini golf course and trace the numbers on the flags.

START

Keep going!

3

4

Weeeee!

8

9

10

You made it!

FINISH

Trace the numbers on the plane's banner, from first to last.

Trace the numbers on the cars, starting with number 1.

Now count backwards from the last car to the first.

Starting at player number 1, draw the route the ball will take as it's passed to each player in number order. Then, draw the ball in the net - GOAL!

Help Bear with his rocket countdown.
Trace the numbers from 5 to 1.

BLAST OFF!

Draw Owl's path as she hops up
the roofs to house number 10.

START

Owl wants to count backwards to house number 1. Trace the roofs from 10 to 1 to help her.